Little theatres

Little theatres
(teatriños)

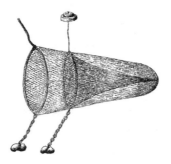

---

or/ou
aturuxos calados

---

poems/poemas
por
Erín Moure

---

with quotes from
Elisa Sampedrín
on Little theatres

ANANSI

Published in 2005 by
House of Anansi Press Inc.
110 Spadina Avenue, Suite 801
Toronto, ON, M5V 2K4
Tel. 416-363-4343
Fax 416-363-1017
www.anansi.ca

Distributed in Canada by
HarperCollins Canada Ltd.
1995 Markham Road
Scarborough, ON, M1B 5M8
Toll free tel. 1-800-387-0117

Distributed in the United States by
Publishers Group West
1700 Fourth Street
Berkeley, CA 94710
Toll free tel. 1-800-788-3123

Permission is gratefully acknowledged to reproduce the following:
(front cover) "Cabeceira," by artist and ethnologist Xaquín Lorenzo Fernández, 1930,
© Museo do Pobo Galego, Santiago de Compostela, Galicia
(back cover) "Placenta," by Galician artist, poet, performer, and editor Antón Lopo,
© 2004 Antón Lopo

10 09 08 07 06   2 3 4 5 6

LIBRARY AND ARCHIVES CANADA CATALOGUING IN PUBLICATION DATA

Mouré, Erin, 1955–
Little theatres / Erin Mouré.

Poems.
ISBN 0-88784-728-5

I. Title.

PS8576.O96L48 2005   C811'.54   C2005-900649-8

Cover design: Bill Douglas at The Bang
Front-cover image: Xaquín Lorenzo Fernández
Back-cover image: Antón Lopo
Photograph on page 94 ("Campo da festa"): Erín Moure
Typesetting: Brian Panhuyzen

 Canada Council **Conseil des Arts**
for the Arts **du Canada**

ONTARIO ARTS COUNCIL
CONSEIL DES ARTS DE L'ONTARIO

We acknowledge for their financial support of our publishing program the Canada Council for the Arts, the Ontario Arts Council, and the Government of Canada through the Book Publishing Industry Development Program (BPIDP).

Printed and bound in Canada

En tout cas, toujours *voix*, et non pas « *vox significativa* », non pas l'ordre signifiant, mais *ce timbre du lieu où un corps s'expose et se profère*.

Contents

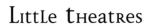

Little theatres

aturuxos caLaDos

Shirred up, wet against the grain

silica might call out

                    its finger to the chest

pressed me still :

That day we passed between the two Toledos

anos annals années a-néantes espidas pido pidas

: rain's hoof-marks

Horses shirred sleeping in wet fields

Regard a tree.

Who would have better seized light's longing?

Longing a labour is first, is first.

First the cold path of it. (Bring water.) Egregious

       is a few steps over wet stones

       ai ailala

       or you might miss it

That limitless strophe

: month

Sage   or wary

Physically   song's capacity

obriga cargada

onérous

these days.

na hortiña do espello (¿espello?)

espiñas

as espiñas dos borrachos do neón

os borrachos do comprensible, do entendemento

estendido

ningures

o son   aire   rumor

en consecuencia

moi poucas palabriñas

cortesías

menos as poldras do pensamento,

empurradas do lonxe.

para María do Cebreiro

Did I have seized ruckus

Job's weir

     catching (outcome) these fishes

     and old leaves

me in the mill house at La Chaux

it all broken down, stone pushed into

auga agua eaux

Writing's 'succumb' with great

           happiness.

in this mere garden (arden-t tend-ing)

mere oars

roars of the drunkards of n-eon

slaked on the understandable, understanding

ex-tended

now-here

sound   air   murmur^{rumour}

In consequence,

very few doting-words

(instead) courtesies

minus the mares of th-inking

ef-faced from the a-far

In little theatres, there are but faces. Boots are faces, a table is a face, the grass stem has an expression that is facial. When Lévinas said "the face is not of the order of the seen" he was making the right connection, but backward. All of what is seen are faces.

Elisa Sampedrín, 1991

Homeⁿaxes á auɕa

Homenaxe ao mineral básico de borscht

Na remolacha hai algo de terra.
Algo de humidade
Algo de humildade
algo mineral. E auga.
A remolacha é depósito de auga.
Recipiente de auga
sangue de terra
sangue de cultivo
sangue azul de tanto encarnado.

Tiven remolacha
cando tiven corpulencia
cando fun solo de terra
errando pola terra para terme

auga.
Humedecerme nas remolachas.
Cor da miña cor.
Coquetería do meu coração.

para Marja Grędysz

Homaçes to Water

Homage to the Basic Mineral of Borscht

In the beet there is something of earth.
Something of humidity
Something of humility
something mineral. And water.
The beet is a reservoir of water.
Container of water
earth-blood
blood cultivated
blue-blooded from so much carmine.

I had beet
when I had corpulence
when I was loam of the earth
wandering the earth so as to hold

water.
To saturate myself in beets.
Colour of my colour.
Shy coquetry of my coeur.

for Marja Grędysz

Homenaxe ao mineral do repolo

No repolo hai algo de voo aterrado
Algo de ceo
Atrás as ás do repolo, que están dobradas
e sobredobradas para aterralo,
repousan aínda máis ás, pensando no ceo.

Hai algo inconsciente no repolo.

Niso, o repolo tamén ten auga, auga de tormenta,
augas do ceo.
O repolo repleto de líquido.
A súa tapa tormentada que non te desmente.

¡Coidado da cabeza se miras o repolo!
Pensamentos das follas pálidas
cortadas na auga fervida.
Hai algo de votivo
de cansazo inmenso
de mirada nunca acabada no espazo dunha vida
pero dobrada e redobrada e sobredobrada
para tapar esas augas tormentadas
augas caladas
augas auguradas
do repolo compartidas con nós, cos seres.

Homage to the Mineral of Cabbage

In the cabbage there is something of flight grounded,
something of sky
Past the wings of the cabbage, which are folded
and folded over to ground it,
lie more wings, pensive with heaven.

There is something unconscious in the cabbage.

In this, the cabbage too holds water, storm water,
waters from on high.
The cabbage complete with liquid.
Its fierce covering that does not deny you.

Watch out for your head if you look at a cabbage!
What the pale leaves must be thinking,
cut into boiling water.
There is something votive
something of immense fatigue
of a gaze never ended in the space of a lifetime
but folded and refolded and folded over
to cap those stormy waters,
deepstruck waters
aquatic auguring
of the cabbage shared with us, with beings.

Homenaxe ao mineral da cebola (I)

Na cebola, hai
algo de lume. Ese lume que se chama
Néboa. A cebola é a maneira
que ten a néboa de entrar na terra.

No solo. Polas follas verdes da cebola.

Mira como as súas follas se estenden no aire.
Mira como, unha vez cortada,
unha folla de cebola ten aire dentro.

O aire é a xenerosidade da néboa.
Coa néboa, hai xenerosidade na terra.
Son dous pensamentos xemelgos.

Son dous pensamentos que sosteñen a terra.
Nestes días bélicos que prometen guerras,
mira como lle axuda a cebola á néboa
a soster a terra.

Homage to the Mineral of the Onion (I)

In the onion, there's
something of fire. That fire known as
Fog. The onion is the way
fog has of entering the earth.

Into the soil. Through the green leaves of the onion.

Look how its leaves extend up into the air.
Look how, once cut,
an onion's leaf has air inside it.

Air is the generosity of fog.
With fog, there is generosity on earth.
These two thoughts are identical.

They are two thoughts that sustain the earth.
In these bellicose days that promise wars,
look how the onion helps fog
to sustain the earth.

Homenaxe á cebola (II)

A cebola tamén é a maneira
na que o solo comparte a terra
co lume.

Polas follas de cebola pasan cantos
dende a terra até o lume.
O lume, xa sabes, é a néboa.
E os cantos —
ruídos dos pés cando pisan o solo.

Pero soamente (admito) se os pés estan calzos
con botas de traballo, de goma.
Nunca cos pés calzos con botas de soldado.

Se os pés estan calzos nesas botas, de soldado,
pechan as follas.
E o canto vai para terra, onde deita
para sempre.
E a néboa cámbiase en tiros
para desaparecer.
E as cen fazulas de cebola aloumiñan as tebras do chan.

Homage to the Onion (II)

The onion is also the way
soil shares the earth
with fire.

Through the leaves of the onion, songs pass
from earth up to the fire.
Fire, as you know, is fog.
And the songs —
the noise of feet when they step upon soil.

But only (I admit) if the feet are clad
in work boots, gum boots.
Never with feet clad in boots worn by soldiers.

If the feet are clad in such boots, of soldiers,
the leaves clam up.
And the song goes into the earth, where it lies
forever.
And the fog turns itself into gunshots
so as to disappear.
And the hundred cheeks of the onion press the cup of the ground.

Homenaxe á potencia da pataca

Nas patacas atopamos unha mestura (moi salvaxe)
de auga e lume
dentro da terra.
É a mestura a máis concentrada
no planeta.
Mesmo nas fábricas de pólvora non se pode mesturar
auga e lume.

Por iso, a potencia revolucionaria das patacas
é máis grande cá da pólvora.
En efecto,
para aumentar a potencia da pólvora, precísanse

magnolias.
Cando fala alguén de pólvora e magnolias
a mensaxe implícita é a da potencia das patacas.
Auga e lume.
Augardente sólido.
Sen canseira.
Mar sen naufraxio.
Tiro sen ferida.

para X. L. Méndez Ferrín

Homage to the Force of the Potato

In potatoes we find a mixture (untamed)
of water and fire
inside the earth.
It's the most concentrated mixture
on the planet.
Even in gunpowder factories, they can't mix
water and fire.

Because of this, the revolutionary force of potatoes
is greater than that of gunpowder.
In fact,
to augment the force of gunpowder, they need

magnolias.
When someone speaks of gunpowder and magnolias
the implicit message is that of the force of potatoes.
Water and fire.
Solid firewater.
Relentless.
Sea without shipwreck.
Gunfire without wound.

for X. L. Méndez Ferrín

Himno ao allo (sen auga)

No allo hai auga sen auga.
En cada dentiño de allo
hai unha soa bágoa
Agardando un ollo.

O seu ollo.

O ollo que perdeu ela
nun momentiño despistado

cando del caeu.

Unha soa bágoa caída é suficiente
para lagrimar a terra.

Se a ollas   *caer.*
Se ves algo   *caer.*
Se podes, á fin e ó cabo,

iso, iso,   *ver.*

Anthem to Garlic (without Water)

In garlic there is water without water.
In each tiny tooth of garlic
is a single tear
Awaiting an eye.

Its own eye.

The eye it lost
in a moment of distraction

when it fell down.

A single tear, fallen, is enough
to tearstain the earth.

If you can see it   *flee.*
If you see something   *flee.*
If, finally and at last, you are able

this, this   *to see.*

Soidade

Sempre na miña vida fáltame, fáltoume, algo,
un alento.
Desde sempre debo aprendelo
da terra.

Eu quería, para agradecerlle á terra
o seu alento,

ser laranxa.
Cerca das cenorias.
Para quentarme no solo.

Sempre na miña vida envexaba eu a cenoria.
¿Como podía algo tan laranxa sentir a tristeza?
¡É laranxa se ben que nunca ve o ceo!

Ser laranxa, polo menos unha vez,
e nunca máis vivir coas tristuras.
Ceibarme destas, por fin
e tocar o solo coa miña cara,

escoitar o alento da terra.

Soidade

All my life I've had a tough time
breathing.
I get scared and feel alone,
me and the earth.

Which me is it talking in the first person?
Should I get up? But I want to lie down.

Sometimes
all I have is water gulped with air
and cut into every membrane.

I try not to let it make me sad. I just say
(which me is it talking in the first person?)
that as long as a carrot can be orange,

I'm going to be orange too.
I'm not going to live with sadnesses.
But free myself, *céibome das tristuras da vida mesma,*
and touch my face to the soil,

and breathe with the breathing of the earth.

I used to think that audiences craved little theatres. They needed just *that much* gesture. A shadow of a hand, a look across a desert; a table with no one there. They've eaten, they've left. Or they didn't come. They got off at another station and went back, there was a war, they lost possessions, the child died of meningitis, the water was putrid, there was no water, the road was blocked; they couldn't come. The schoolteacher was face-down in the ditch. The message didn't arrive. And now the audience is watching. But it's over. The play starts now: after it's over.

Elisa Sampedrín, 1983

eɪɢʜᴛ Lɪᴛᴛʟe ᴛʜᴇᴀᴛʀᴇs of ᴛʜᴇ Cᴏʀɴɪᴄᴇs

by Elisa Sampedrín

Theatre of the Green Leira (Mandúa)

Is bad weather coming
how would we know
Is bad weather coming
call everyone

I am all alone cutting the grass or grain
cutting the wood I am alone
splitting it open carrying it to the crib
Call everyone, put the white table out in the yard
sharpen the knives the scythes
bring out the books now
sharpen the clock's knives too

where did we read any of this
my heart mad with beating
I might lie down here in this field before you come

call everyone
the flies are singing their hymnal hum hum ai ai
how would we know

the needles of the clock are cutting down the names of the hours

Theatre of the Stone Chapel (Abades)

In one of its cornices are the two boots of a man
In one of the stone canzorros
If you listen you can hear him walk
His walk is stone and
his gasoline is stone
and his quill is stone

that's why he hasn't written
because his quill is stone

that's why he hasn't come yet
his gasoline is stone

that's why at night you hear him walking
his boots are stone

even his field of corn is stone
and his mother is water

Theatre of the Hope of a Cebola (Santiso)

On the hill there is no hay
but rain

no hay for a hayrick but
small rivulets singing the grass down

An onion has toppled off a high cart
the chest of the high cart has gone on past the hill

if pressed with a shoe an onion toppled
may take root

Will a shoe ever find it
how can we know

will the onion find a mouth to eat it
how can we ever know

In the channels of water :
small blue rivulets of blue

Theatre of the Millo Seco (Botos)

I am in the little field of my mother
Her field touches
oaks of the valley
and I touch the faces of my corn

Opening corn's faces
so that my hands touch its braille letters
The face of corn is all in braille
the corn wrote it

Fires will burn this evening
burn the dry husks of the corn
and I will learn to read
Sheep will wait by the trough
for they know corn's feature, corn's humility

corn's dichten

grain's

granite too

Theatre of the Stones that Ran (Fontao, 1943)

At night in the valley of penedos erguidos
a glint of wolfram

the uncles' job at night
to touch the glint of wolfram

wolfram brought riches for all in Fontao
they all had jobs then in Fontao
even the prisoners worked in Fontao
the garrison eyed everyone

there was only the night left

The uncles mined the glint in the river course
and stood up in the water
at night they worked each with small hands of xeo
and stood up in the water
climbed out of the river with the wolfram

penedos erguidos
human uncles, tiny

and they ran

for M. I.

Theatre of the Peito (Santiso)

In a woman's arms lies a man
his skin is blue and his lips are blue
and his chest is a hayrick
flat with forks of blue
Perhaps he is dead, perhaps he is dreaming
perhaps he remembers the law has smote him down

he has shut his eyes
his eyes are open
his chest is a hayrick
His head is very tiny, bearded with thread

his head has the breadth of an onion
in a mother's arms
where is she carrying this onion :
its chest is so huge!
on the road above the house roofs :

why is this onion passing by?

Theatre of the Confluence (A Carixa)

A little river and a big river
the story of the bronchials
Some of earth's heartbeat but not all

The water rose in the little river
and washed the big river away
Some of the lungs' telluric memory

The story of a river mouth
and a confluence
From such a place you can hear the river
or you can breathe
but you have to choose or it chooses you

If it chooses you you are an asthmatic
Now you can live here forever
You can sit under the oak leaves and feel wet spray

The big river and the little river
The story of breath in a meander

The big river and the little river
A little story of leaves the river swept away

Theatre of the Calzada (Reboredo)

Nowhere yet has a footfall proven
adequate to its situation
Waiting for the boots to call out
from their stall by the door

Boots wet with river and a field's muck
Boots that touched a swollen sheep
lain there and a swollen yellow cat
lain there rain in its hair
little rivulets running down its body
its hair in wet swirls

Boots that found it there beside the road's calzada
A little grass grown round it far too soon
and no one to bring it to the earth again
though it touches the earth

and the boots touch the earth
that's all they do
touch the earth
that's all they do

eLisa Sampedrín,
some bits
on LittLe tHeatres

W hen we first considered little theatres, we soon found ourselves obliged to throw down our costumes and our masks and make-up. We had to speak all the languages, even made-up ones. It was hard at first seeing these languages take charge, even frightening a bit. Later we stepped into them like water. In fact, that's all there's time for. Little theatres is short; the protagonist doesn't have very much time to protagonize.

from an interview in the Faro de Vigo, 1981

*

The protagonist in little theatres is most often language itself. And it has little time to act. That's the nature of little theatres.

from an interview in the Faro de Vigo, 1981

*

Little theatres is the only theatre definitively preceded in time by film. It tries therefore not to replace film, not to code film, or to take its codes from film, but to fill a space that film misses. Misses nearly entirely.

before a performance, Montreal, 1984

*

I'm not going to write a book about little theatres!

*

In little theatres, everything that happens actually takes place. There's real grass, a real cart making a noise, an axle, an arm, fingers. For this reason, the theatre itself is often empty; the action is so quickly over. The only unreal thing is the proscenium, and this the audience thinks will show them what they have come to see.

overheard by a stagehand,
talking to a journalist at Teatro Fausto, Aberdeen, 1984

*

Still, little theatres doesn't try to make claims for reality. It doesn't have time to do more than enact small fissures in time. It seems a bit credulous at first. The corpse lies down like a corpse. That's reality. But then it gets up again, suddenly, realizing it has forgotten to turn out the light. When the corpse lies down for the last time to be a corpse, we don't actually see it. The whole theatre is dark. This is how reality presents itself in little theatres. We see a corpse sitting up and, then, decisively, not regretfully at all, getting up to turn the light off.

1987

*

When Peter Brook says "Beckett" he speaks of *theatre machines*. Little theatres is a small machine. But not infinitely small. Finite. A small machine. Finite. Small.

*

Just because there are bookstores, you think people read. But look what they read. This is not reading. Which is why I say that little theatres is urgent because people have stopped reading altogether.

Théâtre Méduse, 1981

*

Little theatres doesn't have just one way of dealing with the alphabet. The register, or *rexistro*, of each letter is allowed to move on its own.

*

Some say little theatres has given up on the human body. I say: almost given up on the human body. Or maybe I can put it this way: little theatres does not intend anything about the human body. In fact, the actors feel a bit caught out, to be there taking up so much room while the play is going on.

*

So even the grass has a voice in little theatres. While the actor is talking or moving, you can hear it grow. It is not less important in little theatres. It is, perhaps, in small gestures outside the actors where the real "ideas" of little theatres germinate. This sound of grass, for example. When else have there been theatres for the sound of grass?

*

But the grass can't grow without the body of the actor either. That's the ecology of little theatres at work.

*

Because if we are after *life*, it is not going to be found on a stage. That is why little theatres has decided to be as short as possible. There is no role. Or the role is over before it becomes a role.

Salão Quimera, Lisboa, 1990

*

In little theatres, the stone is about as stony as it can get without making the public's head suffer a blow. There's no mist of origins. Once the stone is stony, the play is done. The stone is stony. Do you get it? Why are you still sitting there?

*

In little theatres the search for form is abandoned. This is its form.

*

Little theatres does not mess with the "dramatic fact of a mystery." It does not try to finish the audience's sentences.

*

Some have said little theatres is minimalist. But this is not strictly so. Whatever else is stripped away in minimalism, and so much, I guess, is indeed "stripped away," a rhetorical convention remains. But rhetoric takes time, and it is time that has been stripped away from little theatres, as it has been from life.

*

Critics have said little theatres is unsatisfactory, primarily this, unsatisfactory. But this is like saying the alphabet is unsatisfactory. Do you expect the alphabet to come up with words for you?

*

When Emmanuel Lévinas said "alterity is strangeness" he might have been talking about little theatres. But he could just as well have said "alterity is alterity" or "strangeness is strangeness." Little theatres is not afraid of this.

*

In little theatres, the protagonist is often alone. Sometimes she leaves the stage. Sometimes not. The actors appear to be interacting only with materials, not with each other. The actor or actress is, in a sense, a costume. Empty of what other theorists have called "soul." The word "soul," in fact, does not apply in little theatres.

1981

*

When the platform of the speaker is raised above, or extended back in space from, the listener, the deployment of power, too, is extended. Its ownership, at the same time, condenses. Politicians make use of this movement every day. But it has worn out its place in the theatre. Theatre has to be a place where something else occurs. Little theatres tries to enact this, to expose a different sort of place, without ownership: an autopia in the sense not of automaton but of autism. Something is demonstrated, yes. But the relation to power is not the same.

overheard on the Toronto subway, 4 April 1999

*

Little theatres is not, strictly speaking, the visible, but is a space that may make sensory cognition possible. Isn't this what we call the visible? I don't believe in a holy theatre; I guess you could say that I wish to leave the invisible alone.

*

It has been noted by some who have lived in times of war that little theatres can be watched in the time it takes to realize a missile is landing. There's a flash, the theatre takes place, the noise occurs. An impossible noise, and the building falls. A grandmother is dead, a son has no leg. But we have seen the theatre. It took place. It did not have time to rescue us.

*

"We criticized her for her corduroys, her semitic nose, her ear bangle. We said she was out of touch with the times. We didn't listen to Elisa Sampedrín in 1984; we didn't listen to her in 1991; we forgot about her in 1995, and we spoke against her in 1997. We were in error, really. We might yet profit from listening to her now."

Erín Moure, 2004

Theatre needs hope in order to survive at the end of the millennium. This has often been said. But little theatres makes do with very little hope. It may be that of all the theatres, little theatres alone will pass over the frontier into the next millennium. Its passage may allow other theatres to follow. It's my hunch that in the next millennium, at least in its first years, hope is not going to count for much. That's when we'll most need little theatres. It's very conservative in its use of hope as fuel.

Elisa Sampedrín
Vigo, 1998

Late Snow of May — poemas de auga —

A gramática do can

Teño un pequeniño can de auga
É soamente unha cavilla pequena
o meu can de auga

¿Velo
tan esgotado
atrás da leira
co fociño acochado na herba dobrada?

É o meu can de auga.
Cada folla de herba molla unha bufanda na súa pasaxe.

Mesma a herba hoxe está correndo.
Mesma a herba hoxe toca o can de auga.

The grammar of the dog

I have a little dog of water
It is just a little peg
my dog of water

Do you see it
so worn down
across the little field
nosing low in the bended grasses?

It is my dog of water.
Each leaf of grass dips a scarf into its passing.

Even the grass today is running.
Even the grass today touches the dog of water.

O amor do can

Amo un pequeniño can de auga
Das leiras vén na miña fiestra

É soamente unha cavilla pequena
o meu can de auga

¿Víchelo
na herba e por riba das follas
co seu temperamento?

É o meu can de auga.
Mira como toca o cristal.

The love of the dog

I love a little dog of water
From the field it comes into my window

It is just a little peg
my dog of water

Did you see it
in the grass and on the leaves
with its temperament?

It is my dog of water.
Look how it touches the glass.

Agarimo de maio

Casei hoxe cunha gata de auga.
Debía casar con ela, Chámoume.
Casei con ela coa cara erguida ao ceo.

Foi neste momento que vin o pardál,
co seu ombro mouro, agarrando o bico do brelo.

Foi neste momento que vin a historia da neve
máis alta cá rama.

Onde a nube estivo máis branquiña e máis fría,
nevaba.

Neste intre, casei coa gata de auga.
A miña cara pegada ao espazo onde xa acabou
espazo, Espazo de espazo, baleiro, o aér.

Agarimo, May

Today I married a cat of water.
I had to marry her, She called.
I married her with my face upright to the sky.

That's when I saw the sparrow with
its black shoulder, gripping the branch end.

That's when I saw the history of snow
high above the branch.

Where the cloud was whitest and coldest,
it was snowing.

That's when I married the cat of water.
My face pressed to the space where space had only just
ended, Space of space, empty, ô air.

Ancient memory of May

Don't you wish sometimes there were
a darkness
for a word like this?

There's sweet air trilling in the window
such little leaves of May
so many jaggedy edges.

When I cut them out of paper
                you were sleeping.
When I hung them on the birch branches
                you were already sleeping.

Shall we go together to the field
seeking graves that are full of sound?

One of us came back from there,
earlier,
much earlier,
a single footpath in the snow.

for Emma, 17 May 2002

Recordo antigo de maio

¿Quixeras ás veces que fose
unha escuridade
pra unha palabra como esta?

Airexes doces trilan pola fiestra
follas tan pequenas de maio
tantos bordos dentadiños.

Cando as recortei dun papel
durmiches.
Cando as pendín nos brelos do bidueiro
xa estabas durmindo.

¿Iremos xuntas ás leiras
buscando sepulturas cheas de sons?

Unha de nós xa chegou de alí,
máis cedo,
moito máis cedo,
un só camiño na neve.

para Emma, 17 maio 2002

Ora, a solidão, ainda vai ter de aprender muito para saber o que isso é, Sempre vivi só, Também eu, mas a solidão não é viver só, a solidão é não sermos capazes de fazer companhia a alguém ou a alguma coisa que está dentro de nós, a solidão não é uma árvore no meio duma planície onde só ela estaja, é a distância entre a seiva profunda e a casca, entre a folha e a raiz.

José Saramago, O Ano da Morte de Ricardo Reis

aUTOBIOGRaPHIes of SLeep

Did you sing that yellow tune?
Its gouache folds me

Clear water and new shoots
iphigenial

Streets we once mentioned
south street
auburn
written in the book of immigration

whose sleeping face
of awe
            flick
            flicker

Her stream's roar and pageant
flag or stirrup

I rose up and rode that stream

was "I" that fine muscle?
all fibre wriggling against a taut wire
no shoulders but fins

whose waking meant more to me
my waking? yours?

what did it matter; the plasma surfaced
alone and weary

a shook foil   reticular

finger's shimmer
                fabricked and fashioned

light's filtrage
under a door

Did you ever say sleep
its field of sumac and cicada
did you wear down that shirt cuff
to its thread
tracing a path of silent industry

where speech is possible's framework

testing nightly
                hippolyte's girdle
                (the known world)

                light   shadow   dignity   mores

Or ache in such tugged finery
tooth and eye

shut plasticity tonight and
morning

the body frail moves into sexuality's tremble
uncalled, unbidden:

friend friend
I knew you

how I knew you?

In sleep's empathy   *lain down*
sleep's lonely

        four *

   * flower

      * furnace

Some birches also sketch sky
behind cloth's factories
rails now gone

In these fields' paths   immigration has mild joy
walks forth
aspen tremble

Bits of birch
because I as organism bear in me a trace —
memory's trace —

capital's rhizome

Sleep's opposite   could it be
the smell of bread

The mattress that became soil
became limp a body
slept on its own

took on air
folded at the rib

when the plants came
grew soil to this body's soil
this sleep's membrane
colchonada na rúa

for alight

salvo

Lost in sleep's phosphorescence
it's dark here
close to the jaw

where surge's density draws a plasma under
its mouth crooked
lit   resurgent

did disease of the throat marry us?
Caught by the jaw and pulled sideways
gills tugged open

a gash of brilliant carmine
one wing bent back
under me
                one wing risen
                over her

ruckled ruckus
brilliant red

Oblique's emotion set at bay
to dream "defend"
to want this membrane   *held*
"please hold this membrane"

head pushed downward into stream's cold course
as costas
ribs
held in

my hands' motion and rough bay
(cascade   a torrent
                    : no one hears)

may's
wet air
birch

                              (an edifice's
                passages in wet stems ever
                    : no one sees)

the first story of Latin
(os araos)

by Erín Moure

Je sais seulement qu'il faut faire ce qu'il faut pour ne plus être un pestiféré et que c'est là ce qui peut, seul, nous faire espérer la paix. . . . Et c'est pourquoi j'ai décidé de refuser tout ce qui, de près ou de loin, pour de bonnes ou de mauvaises raisons, fait mourir ou justifie qu'on fasse mourir.

Tarrou à Rieux,
Albert Camus, La peste

for Chus Pato and Manuel Igrexas

The First Story of Latin

The hunger we felt before entering the water.
Latin was our language of birth, we
spelled it: L. A. T. I. N.
and it said *language* to us,
we spelled our *language*.
                    Spoke this
as if latin were water and we were entering its ocean
with no turning round.

I'm late, the sky said, but we didn't wait, we didn't
want to. Our language drove us ever in.

"Do you know my latin?"
"Can you read my latin?"
"I am lost in the shadow of my latin."
"My mother's latin is my latin."

So few, speaking latin, have blue eyes.
Of those that do,
it's said they're from high up, far from the ocean,
where the air burnt them white
when first they opened

frost white *brancos coma neve* then azuis, *blue.*

XIIV   Ora e labora

The intent was to never sleep with knives
but to be clothed and belted
bieitiniñas ready to sing out every hour
so one life's oration can save 10M

In case of new bombardments we need more like us
saving lives by refusing to sleep with knives

Well maybe a bit more, maybe corn cutting too

Wind plays the chimneys of Galiza a faint guitar
Would it make you scared slightly too at night
It means rain's coming, auga trying to decipher clouds

In my latin, words have gone missing for centuries now
In my latin, whole letters of the alphabet
can't be read today

In your language can you say mencer ao mencer
Does that mean
dawn at dawn

ah ah
good

premonition works in your language too

Soidade

We call them apagóns in Botos so do I even in my latin
Apagóns remind us we're lonely caverns
Our roof's guitar changed for
a clarinet maybe

For wind invents instruments where it will
Will being a factor here not uniquely human

Water running down the single boats of the grasses
Millions of grasses
Held in cups of leaves then running over
                ailalalá ai ai la la ai la la la ai la

Whole shutters wet now
Whole mysteries contagion glass
ligatures absent
Darkness everywhere water

Here I await light from Fenosa maybe

Lonxe de min

Songstress

"tres tipos de paxaros na horta á mañá
os seus sons cántos sons son cantos aí"

precious little on earth is worth such song
if we make worth a measure

should we
not likely perhaps let's walk instead the
soaked road to Sestelo now rain's finished

rain's fábrica please say it won't rain till t'morrow
rooftiles already scattered down

persons still drenched in the road, its edges washed away
a simple diction will do

tres tipos de paxaros
paxaros non son persoas de pasaxe
e xílgaros non son xentes que
xacen por aquí

Apples

I don't know the old slang for anything here
I only speak latin

What is shoulder in your language?
In my latin it is *shoulder*,
it has two parts, bivalve, one fits in the cadaleito of the other
A bit like a sepulchre but no, not really

Listen to it spread out and upward
Listen to it wave down the roman road

This means laughter
or wings

No no no, not really
That's the same in my language
Really

Light spun in fallen leaves till
blackbirds chunter in that leafless maceira
Never eating one whole apple
¡Pecking every apple in November with a hole!

Auga LI

What part of the poem is description only?
What part is fear.

*Auga fervida toleada tecida mándame cedo as súas canción*s

What part of my house is granite and which
gneiss and how
So much cold radiating in the doorway, cold rain
stone doorway with the postigo wide open

what does that mean in my latin   (dutch door)
some say postizo I know this
I lay down in my latin and hammocked dearly

hat-first a wind took me

estou destapada agora
in my latin: now hatless
hatless in my mother's tongue she worked to learn

having immigrated,
not knowing a word of it

Mergullada

To me your language is so like Latin,
you have ombro and sombra
how similar

in my latin it's shoulder and shadow
can you see it's working?

I'm soon going to learn your language
miolo and ollo
marrow and eye

Ho! I'd better learn it quickly
before it moves on like water

ollomol moi mollado
oficio fio dos fieis
afiador

Agradecemento

In fact I am losing my latin for your latin
I am letting my latin fall away
It is a glass of rain I can no
longer drink from it
It is a leaf of paper I can no longer
be its tree

Birds fly out of its branches in gusts and into chapapote,
into the piche, my errancy errando o noso error

With such a latin we can work aloud together

I would like my latin to feel joy's companion
and begin to speak
latin once more

If I want to speak to birds
should I use latin or latin
my mother's idiom or yours

My mother's idiom she invented on arrival
             or
Aturuxos calados
Oídos en ningures, oídos desde aquí

UIIX

These days can you too feel the sorrow of latin
Can you feel latin's sorrow or weir
through royaume or reino

or kingdom
or ferida's fury
which comes to an end with rain's commencement

its arms of water that can brave an ocean
"tocada por el manto negro de la asfixia"*

a paper coat against such darkened rain
and blue grass sandals
worn while the sea is dreamed
and shutters

barred tight against this rain
My latin in darkness is water's idiom:

o goberno mándanos de calarmos
e nunca calaremos
berramos coa forteleza dunha vaga, unha onda-bágoa
our sleeves of paper that let wind reign

---

* Even *El Mundo*, 2 Dec 2002, the right-wing paper largely the voice of the Partido Popular,
found words to loyally describe the *marea negra* from the Prestige disaster while not saying
"marea negra" — black tide. Instead they called it "the black mantle of asphyxiation."

Subxunctivo do futuro

There are several ways to avoid war
Drying corn on stalks is one
To feed pigs on small chestnuts is another
Just listening is a third

One other, also
Lauerd, for yure pite ye gete vs fra sinne

I don't think it's working
In my latin we tend to disabuse fate, we
listen to TV news
Really listen
Inoculate ourselves daily till we don't know death

In your language what do you call this

In my idiom
defende vs fra envie & hateredin
shadow of those jets and armament defending
"us" for petroleum

what 250M persons might do for good
but they *sal meke* troops of them

Soño nórdico

Far off, rains tumble into the fields at Sestelo too
From one spot you can see the belltower
I'm not there I'm in Botos but the mind's eye

says belltower,
the mill's river full not turning its stone
the water passing unimpeded
stone on its side in the current below

boys pushed it maybe
or it fell
or the dono of the mill emigrated

In my latin I can dream north across the waters of Biscaia
no one answers
Or walk that stone road to the commune of *Lignières Orgères*
romans built it
Romans irrevocable invasion and the celtic kings
who did eat yew to refuse capitulation
It rained every minute, thought got wetter
Others said so too

romans built it
So I do believe

for Lani

Symmetry

Sempre is not a word to be used lightly
Not in the latin I know
For this we need a language that rings of water

Agasallo cortesía pataca amor

Passing over stones or off the roof tiles
Carrying red soil from the leiras down past the shut mill
Running into windows and soaking curtains
Slow charcos spreading under the doors
continents adrift

(e un petroleiro afundido no mar)

Me in green gum boots knee-dry
yes now I remember
In the picture that's me *agasallo cortesía*
I think so
wearing such high shoes *pataca amor*

UIX

What if I spoke every hour in Latin
Dreamed red cows a rope looped on each horn
Woke up hearing my mother who spoke this latin
your latin is my latin I did tell her
I never spoke the vulgate tongue

To roll in rough sleep feeling cold ever
Botos cows passing under my window
red boned backs sway and step slow upward
Three sheep too
my face in the window just awakened

two years later the same sheep *ai ai ola bo día que tal*

Fall of water constant in my camiño
dogs barking at chickens and what else who knows
wind and leaves
armistice
castigation's burnt library

Two sides of the glass are waiting clearly
Two shores two roads two ataúdes
eyhe marja eyje aiai o meu amor
My mother's latin a blank voice out of memory

I learned it from her
I could learn it more

Habeus Corpus

I think we both have the right of habeus corpus
in my latin and in yours

Corn on its stalk anyway
Perhaps a leira of dry corn
ordinary folks shucking this corn for cows

Yesterday I walked down the street of wheelbarrows
the whole street said *carreta carreta*

But my father was never shut in prison
My brothers are old and eat at home
My grandfather never died at thirty
leaving a small father, tiny tiny

Carreta carreta

The right to have the body

one ran away to Oporto or París
one sent a card franqueado *Bos Aires*
one was buried at night with spades

it could be "that very corn"

MMII

Previously we received exemptions for grammar to
enable new structures
A whole book of hours could be built on the Verb
But not its subjunctive,

from this mode the "future" has vanished
and is no longer advised

Enough doubt is already established by government
Elected by small votes and tyrannical thereafter
Leaving us, they say, the preterito
for describing our inner selves

But who marked the cross on that voting paper
Who just scraped at a name
Who wrote in *I don't think you're listening
to any of us*

Now that's saying it straight in latin

There are no young men in this village I notice
No young women

No lights at this very moment
You can hear it everywhere the sound of water

Even I am too old for use in war

Exchange of Vows

Latin was ever a bit of my dexterity
I learned it young and tried it often
I am not yet so dexterous in yours

I meant agasallo you said gift
we said amizade I said embarrassed

but that was in my latin, you said see you tomorrow
until then or until later
até logo

I knew what you were saying as if
you too spoke latin

we both suddenly spoke latin
¡Latin was where we first met our mothers!

I was so glad of my *later*
with its two verticals and echo of até logo
yours too has two verticals
letters like penedos

até logo I said to you too

Throat and Weir

When I left the world, I left a bigger latin
This my epitaph prepared already
ink wet written once by birds

But not an epitaph for
I only want to be alive in latin
my "but" a part of speech in latin

for I want to put the seal of joy
on latin
My circumstance
of throat and weir
can we discuss it in your latin
if I listen
can we discuss it in your latin now
if I only listen
se vos escoito pola primeira vez

Que pracer oír o voso latín
Dame graza escoitar o voso latín
Que maxestade
Que toca fresca ailala do mar

Araos

Do you see how it works now
I speak to you and you speak to me

paxaro   arao

When you speak to me in latin
I listen for latin and in latin
then I speak to you *paxaro   arao*
and I am speaking latin too

Such a pained way of coming into language
your linguaxe
opening my throat our entry
(un petroleiro afundido no mar)
(e o mar doente de carbón)

Now we must stop to wipe the spilled oil off birds
In your latin they are paxaros or araos
I must urgently adopt your latin

the word arao in the linguaxe

paxaro   arao
paxaro   arao

In my latin now they are araos too

There's a moment at which what we call the end and the beginning cross paths. It's very brief. The end had already come to this, then the curtain goes up: it begins. Or maybe the words don't even apply. Even the word "curtain," what is it? It moves in the rain. That's the moment of little theatres.

ES

Diccionario / Dictionary

a

afiador	knife-sharpener (tradesman)
afundido (*pp.m.* of *inf.* afundir)	sunk
agarimo	affection
agasallo	gift
agradecmento	act of thanking
aloumiñar (*inf.*)	to caress
amizade	friendship
amor	love
ano	year
apagón	power blackout
aquí	here
arao	common murre or guillemot (rare seabird in Spain)
ataúde	coffin
até logo	till later, see you later
aturuxos	spontaneous whoops in a song
auga	water
azul (*pl.* azuis)	blue

b

berramos (*1st pers.pl.* of *inf.* berrar)	we shout
bieitiniña	Benedictine nun (dim.)
borrachos	drunks
branco	white

c

cadaleito	coffin
caderno	notebook
caer (*inf.*)	to fall
calados (*pp.m.pl.* of *inf.* calar)	silent, deep
calzada	road surface, asphalt
canto	canto, song
cánto	how many
canzorro	stone carving near roof
carreta	wheelbarrow (and a street in Compostela)
cebola	onion

cedo — early
ceibar *(inf.)* — to set free
chapapote — oil spill contamination
charcos — puddles
cortesía — courtesy

d
desde — from (in space or time)
destapado/a *(pp. of inf.* destapar) — uncovered
dichten (Ger.) — the spoken, poetry
doente — aching, sore, hurting
dono — owner

e
empurrada *(pp.f. of inf.* empurrar) — pushed
entendemento — understanding (n.)
erguido *(pp.m. of inf.* erguer) — standing up
espello — mirror
espido — naked
espiña — thorn
estendido *(pp.m. of inf.* estender) — extended

f
fábrica — factory
falamos *(1st pers.pl. of inf.* falar) — we speak/talk, are speaking/talking
Fenosa — electrical monopoly in Galiza
ferida *(pp.f. of inf.* ferir) — wounded
fervido/a *(pp. of inf.* fervir) — fervid/boiling
fiel *(pl.* fieis) — loyal
franqueado *(pp.m. of inf.* franquear) — postmarked

h
hortiña — kitchen garden, potager (dim.)

l
leira — cultivated field or plot of land
lonxe — far away

m

maceira	appletree
man	hand
mañá	morning, tomorrow
mar	sea
mencer	dawn
menos	minus, less
mergullada (*pp.f.* of *inf.* mergullar)	soaking wet
millo	corn
min	me
mollado (*pp.m.* of *inf.* mollar)	wet

n

neve	snow
ningures	nowhere

o

oficio	trade, office
oído (*pp.m.* of *inf.* oír, *also* ouvido)	heard
ollomol	sea bream
onda	wave (of sea)

p

palabriñas	pl. of *palabra*, words (dim.)
pasaxe	passage
pataca	potato
paxaro	bird
peito	chest, breast
penedo	standing stone
pequeniño	m. of *pequeno*, little (dim.)
persoa	person
petroleiro	oil tanker (ugh)
piche	pitch, sticky oil
pidas (*2nd pers.sing.* of *inf.* pedir)	you ask
pido (*1st pers.sing* of *inf.* pedir)	I ask
poldra	filly
postizo	dutch door

pouco	little
preterito	past perfect tense
r	
reino	realm, kingdom
s	
seco	dry
sempre	forever, always
soidade	loneliness, aloneness, solitude
t	
tebras	darkness, the gloom
v	
vaga	big sea wave, breaker
x	
xacen (*3rd pers.pl.* of *inf.* xacer)	they lie (bodily position)
xente	people, folks
xeo	ice
xílgaros	goldfinches

araos
paxaros

araos
paxaros

(bring water)

Dès que la vérité qu'on croit tirer d'elle s'est fait jour, est devenue la vie et le travail du jour, l'oeuvre se referme en elle-même comme étrangère à cette vérité et comme sans signification, car ce n'est pas seulement par rapport aux vérités déjà sues et sûres qu'elle paraît étrangère, le scandale du monstrueux et du non-vrai, mais toujours elle réfute le vrai : quoi qu'il soit, même s'il est tiré d'elle, elle le renverse. . . .

Et cependant, elle dit le mot commencement. . . .

Mais elle-même ne commence pas.

Maurice Blanchot

acknowledgements

To Liz Kirby, always;

and to Chus Pato and Belén Martín.

Also, for their kindness and xenerosidade during the writing of this work:
Associação Barcas do Minho, Pilar Beiro, Ana Bringas, María do
Cebreiro, Chris Daniels, Anxo Fernández Ocampo, Xesús Fraga, Kim
Fullerton, Xavier Gómez Guinovart, Phil Hall, Stephen Horne,
Guillermo Iglesias Díaz, Manuel Igrexas Rodríguez, Antón Lopo,
Emma M., Lani Maestro, Robert Majzels, Ken Mouré, Museo do Pobo
Galego, Lou Nelson, María Reimóndez, Manuel Rivas, Lisa
Robertson, Elisa Sampedrín, Colette St-Hilaire.

And for support that made this work possible:
- The Canada Council for the Arts, for a senior arts grant
- Manuel and his family, and Chus, for letting me live in the Casa
  de Cuñarro
- Ana Bringas, for the móbil
- Belén, Lúa and Guiller for sharing their home so often

Thanks to the editors of *espasmo* (Galiza), *No: a journal of the arts*
(USA), *Ploughshares* (USA), *La Traductière* (France), *tsé tsé* (Argentina),
The Best American Poetry 2004 (USA), *LRC* (Canada) and *The Malahat
Review* (Canada) for previous appearances of some of these texts.